SILVER LININGS

A Journal for Navigating
Life's Challenges

ANNA KATZ

Bluestreak
BOOKS

⹀Bluestreak

Weldon Owen is a division of Bonnier Publishing USA
1045 Sansome Street, San Francisco, CA 94111
www.weldonowen.com

Edited and designed by Girl Friday Productions
www.girlfridayproductions.com

Written by Anna Katz

Library of Congress Cataloging-in-Publication data is available.

ISBN-13: 978-1-68188-231-4

First Printed in 2017
10 9 8 7 6 5 4 3 2 1
2017 2018 2019 2020

Printed in China

Introduction

The goal of this journal is not to turn your frown upside down. This journal is about being accepted—and accepting yourself—as you are. It's OK to be frustrated when you miss the train, or despairing when you get dumped, or just plain grouchy first thing in the morning. By all means, keep your frown downside down if you want. But—and here's where some effort might be required—can you also, simultaneously, look on the bright side? We're not talking about stuffing your feelings down, down, down, hoping that one day that lump of emotional coal will somehow turn into a diamond. Rather, we're suggesting using a wider lens to look at whatever current challenge you may be facing. Just as that skinned knee you got as a seven-year-old toppling your bike was painful at the time, today it probably doesn't hurt so much. And you learned from that moment. How to get back on your bike, or to roll up your pants so the cloth didn't get caught in the chain. That's not to discount the pain you experienced at the time—that pain was real. But it has diminished, and here you are, riding a bike like a pro.

This can apply to very real, very grown-up, very emotional or psychic pain. Once you get some time and space, it hurts less. (Or it doesn't, and it simply is what it is. Some things just hurt forever.) But if while going through something hard you can look around and within with compassion and curiosity, you can learn something about yourself, about life, about the adult version of falling down and then getting back on that bike again, and again, and again.

Such is the vexing complexity of acceptance: it's OK to hurt, and it's OK to look ahead to when it won't hurt, and it's OK to search for meaning, and it's OK to allow for meaninglessness, and it's hard to do all of that at the same time. This journal is meant to make it a little less hard, to give you tools to help you reflect on what you're experiencing, and what it might mean for your future—a minute or a day or a lifetime from now.

As you go through this journal, you will find opportunities to consider past moments when life handed you lemons, and to think about how you'd like to deal with lemons when they inevitably appear in the future. You will find that some of the prompts and practices are repeated, allowing you to try them more than once. Perhaps your answers or actions will change. Perhaps not. Remember, only you can decide what to keep, what to grow, and what to let go.

Silver Linings: A Journal for Navigating Life's Challenges provides a no-pressure, no-stakes opportunity to examine your life with love. Because with patience, tenderness, and practice, it is possible to make the best of what you have, which isn't always perfect but may be better than you realize. Just as plants need rainstorms to grow, you never do know what possibilities today's clouds might bring.

When a storm's brewing, why not meet it head-on?
Think of something that you're currently worried about.
Now allow that worry to run its course.

....
....
....
....
....
....
....
....

What is the very worst that could happen?

....
....
....
....
....
....
....
....
....
....
....

What is the very best that could happen?

What is the most likely thing to happen?

In the middle of every
difficulty lies opportunity.

*Albert Einstein (1879–1955),
theoretical physicist*

Do you tend to take risks, or do you prefer to play it safe?

What are the benefits of playing it safe? What are the drawbacks?

What are the benefits of taking risks? What are the drawbacks?

What expectations or limitations might you be imposing on
yourself when you play it safe? When you take risks?

Pause and take a deep breath. There's no need to do anything in this moment—everything is OK just as it is.

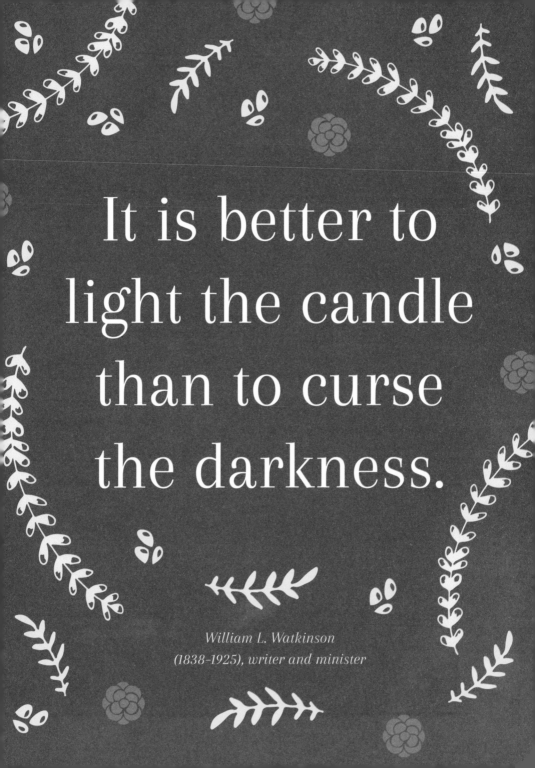

It is better to light the candle than to curse the darkness.

William L. Watkinson
(1838–1925), writer and minister

Sometimes we are able to think before we speak or
weigh our options before we act. And sometimes we aren't.

Write about a time when something bad happened
and you reacted immediately.

....
....
....
....
....
....
....
....
....

Write about a time when something bad happened
and you paused before responding.

....
....
....
....
....
....
....
....
....

Was there any difference in the outcome? Was there a difference in the way you felt about the situation or about yourself afterward?

Think of a challenging time in your life that
ultimately worked out for the best.

What was the most difficult part of it?

_____

_____

_____

_____

_____

_____

_____

_____

_____

What did you feel while you were going through it?

_____

_____

_____

_____

_____

_____

_____

_____

_____

_____

_____

How did the challenges end up changing your life for the better?

_____

_____

_____

_____

_____

_____

_____

_____

_____

_____

_____

_____

_____

_____

_____

_____

_____

_____

_____

_____

_____

_____

_____

Was the outcome better because of the challenges?

This too shall pass.

Persian proverb

Write about a time when you tried and failed.
Did you persevere, or did you give up?

What are the benefits of persevering? What are the drawbacks?

What are the benefits of giving up? What are the drawbacks?

How might you know when persevering could serve you,
or when it might be better to give up?

Next time you feel frustrated,
stop what you're doing and just sit.

Patience is the best
remedy for every trouble.

Plautus (3rd century BCE),
playwright

Write down one *bad* thing that happened today.

Now write down five *good* things that happened today.

It was not facing what life dealt that made you crazy, but rather trying to set life straight where it was unstraightenable.

Anne Lamott (b. 1954), author

Set a timer for five minutes. Sit quietly and take notice of these states: physical, mental, and emotional. Afterward, write about it here.

Physical

Mental

Emotional

When plans go awry, think about the big picture.
Remember the end goal and then work backward—all
you have to do is modify the details.

Obstacles are a part of the journey.

Michelle Obama (b. 1964),
former first lady of the United States

Sometimes life hands us lemons and we make lemonade. Other times life hands us lemons and we end up with plain old lemon juice.

When have you fully surrendered to misfortune?

_____

_____

_____

_____

_____

_____

_____

_____

When have you made the best of a bad situation?

_____

_____

_____

_____

_____

_____

_____

_____

_____

What prompted you to choose one path over the other?

Write down something that was difficult for you today.
Notice how you feel in your body and mind.

Now write down something that you enjoyed today.
Notice how you feel in your body and mind.

Flow with whatever may happen
and let your mind be free. Stay
centered by accepting whatever you
are doing. This is the ultimate.

Zhuangzi (4th century BCE), philosopher

Try to allow all feelings to be present.
Don't resist, ignore, or soothe—just notice.

Write about a time when you took a situation *personally*, when you interpreted an external event as a reflection on your character rather than a consequence of your actions or a random occurrence.

Looking back, what in that situation was beyond your control?
What did you have the power to control?

We may encounter many defeats,
but we must not be defeated.

Maya Angelou (1928–2014), poet

Just because something bad happens, it doesn't need to cloud
the rest of your day. What was the worst thing that happened to you today?

Write down three unexpected positive consequences.

> Not everything that is faced can be changed; but nothing can be changed until it is faced.
>
> *James Baldwin (1924-1987), writer*

Would you rather problem-solve than problem-*feel*? Think of a bad situation. Write about the feelings you had at the time—do not write about the *circumstances* of the situation. If you find yourself getting caught up in the what, how, and why, pause, breathe, and then try to return to the feelings.

Think about a difficult moment in your life when you were experiencing uncomfortable feelings. Set a timer for five minutes and just sit with it. Notice these states: physical, mental, and emotional. Afterward, write about it here.

Physical

Mental

Emotional

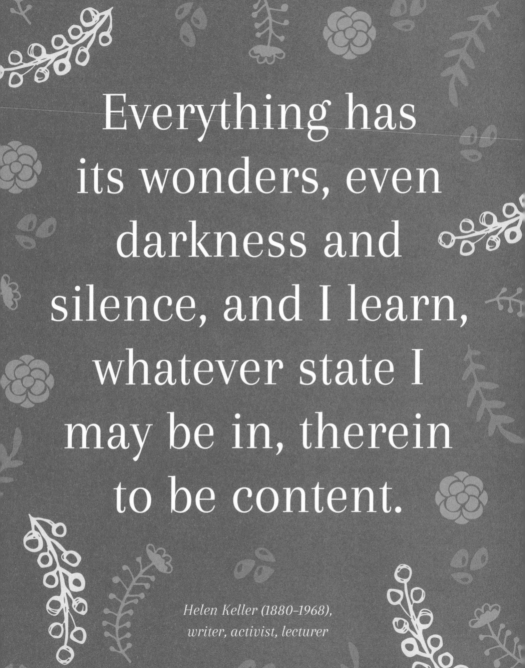

Everything has its wonders, even darkness and silence, and I learn, whatever state I may be in, therein to be content.

Helen Keller (1880–1968), writer, activist, lecturer

Every emotion has a job to do: for example, fear can protect us, sadness can contain us, joy can propel us. What emotion are you experiencing right now, and what job is it doing?

Write down one *bad* thing that happened today.

Now write down five *good* things that happened today.

New beginnings are often
disguised as painful endings.

Laozi (6th century BCE), philosopher

Think of a painful ending—a breakup, losing a job, even the death of a loved one. Did it create some kind of new beginning in your life?

_____

_____

_____

_____

_____

_____

_____

_____

_____

_____

_____

_____

_____

_____

_____

_____

_____

_____

_____

_____

_____

_____

The next time you find yourself worrying, do something with your hands—work in the garden, do the dishes, or play catch with your child or a friend. Getting out of your head and into your body will bring you back to the present.

I make the most of all that comes
and the least of all that goes.

Sara Teasdale (1884-1933), poet

Hard times can reveal the kindness of others. Write about
a difficult time in which someone unexpectedly helped you.

Write down something that was difficult for you today.
Notice how you feel in your body and mind.

Now write down something that you enjoyed today.
Notice how you feel in your body and mind.

Time is a true friend to sorrow.

William Wordsworth
(1770-1850), poet

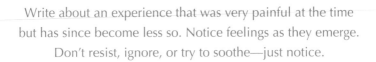

Write about an experience that was very painful at the time
but has since become less so. Notice feelings as they emerge.
Don't resist, ignore, or try to soothe—just notice.

Look back on time with kindly eyes,
He doubtless did his best;
How softly sinks his trembling sun
In human nature's west!

Emily Dickinson (1830–1886), poet

Sometimes a little perspective is the best medicine.
Think back to a time when you were going through something
so horrible that you weren't sure how you'd survive it.

What did you do to get yourself through it?

As your present self, what advice would you give your past self?

_____

_____

_____

_____

_____

_____

_____

_____

_____

_____

If you're currently facing a new challenge, what advice do you
think your future self would give your present self?

_____

_____

_____

_____

_____

_____

_____

_____

_____

_____

_____

There is no good in arguing with the inevitable. The only argument available with an east wind is to put on your overcoat.

James Russell Lowell (1819-1891), poet

Think of something that you're currently worried about.
Now allow that worry to run its course.

What is the very worst that could happen?

What is the very best that could happen?

What is the most likely thing to happen?

People often wait for a "better" time to pursue their interests, whether it's singing or painting or traveling the world. That thing you've been putting off for a better time? Do it now.

He that has no ill luck
grows weary of good luck.

Spanish proverb

Most of us would choose to have good luck all the time, but we need clouds to appreciate sunshine, and sunshine to appreciate clouds. What seemingly opposing situations in your life might actually complement each other? What "negative" might you need in order to appreciate the "positive"?

....

....

....

....

....

....

....

....

....

....

....

....

....

....

....

....

....

....

Write down one *bad* thing that happened today.

....

....

....

....

....

Now write down five *good* things that happened today.

....

....

....

....

....

....

....

....

....

....

....

....

....

....

....

The possibilities are numerous once
we decide to act and not react.

George Bernard Shaw
(1856-1950), playwright

Life would be a lot easier if everyone were just like us, and if we could control other people and their behavior. Of course, the only thing we can control is ourselves—our thoughts and actions. Think back to a time when you and someone else were at odds.

What did you have the power to control in the interaction?
What was beyond your control?

Imagine you could see the same situation through the
other person's eyes. What might be the reasoning behind
their stance? What might be the emotions at play?

Do you tend to focus on who's right
and who's wrong? If so, why? If not, why not?

....

....

....

....

....

....

....

....

....

....

....

In the future, how might you approach a similar interaction? What is your
ideal response to a person who is behaving in a way that you don't like?

....

....

....

....

....

....

....

....

....

....

....

Would you rather be right, or would you rather find a solution? Listen first, and consider your desired outcome before you speak.

Hard times allow you to express the kindness in yourself, and helping others can help you step outside of your own issues and gain a broader perspective. Write about a time when you helped someone who was going through a difficult experience. How did that make you feel?

Think of someone who has been kind to you—a friend, a grandparent, a significant other. The next time you are struggling, imagine what they would say to comfort you. Can you give that same loving acceptance to yourself?

Arrange whatever pieces come your way.

*Virginia Woolf
(1882–1941), writer*

If your life were a story and you were its author, how would
you describe your past? How would you frame it within the greater
context? Write in third person and in novel-like detail.

If your life were a story and you were its author, what would you like the next chapter to be? What would you need to do to turn this story into reality? Write in third person and in novel-like detail.

After joy, grief;
after grief, joy.

Tamil proverb

Make a list of the big events in your life—weddings,
deaths, graduations, births, dreams realized, hopes dashed.
That's it, just a list. Life's full of ups and downs, isn't it?

-
-
-
-
-
-
-
-
-
-
-
-
-
-
-
-
-
-
-
-
-
-
-
-

- ....
- ....
- ....
- ....
- ....
- ....
- ....
- ....
- ....
- ....
- ....
- ....
- ....
- ....
- ....
- ....
- ....
- ....
- ....
- ....
- ....
- ....
- ....
- ....
- ....
- ....

Don't take what happens to you personally. Though you may find a lesson worth learning, most of the time the things that happen to you are not personal.

Do you tend to consider yourself a victim of fate, or
do you feel like you're the master of your own destiny?

What are the benefits of "going with the flow"?
What are the drawbacks?

What are the benefits of being more proactive about creating your life?
What are the drawbacks?

How might your tendencies toward being more proactive or
going with the flow limit you? How might they liberate you?

The next time you catch yourself thinking that something *should* be different than it is, take a moment to think about the big picture. Then do yourself a kindness and cut the word "should" from your vocabulary.

Was I deceiv'd, or did a sable cloud
Turn forth her silver lining on the night?

John Milton (1608–1674), poet

Silver linings aren't always within the sable cloud—sometimes
they are within *you*. Write about something that went wrong recently.

What strengths and skills did you use to deal with it?
Underline the strengths and skills that helped you the most.

....

....

....

....

....

....

....

....

....

....

....

....

....

....

....

....

....

....

....

....

....

....

....

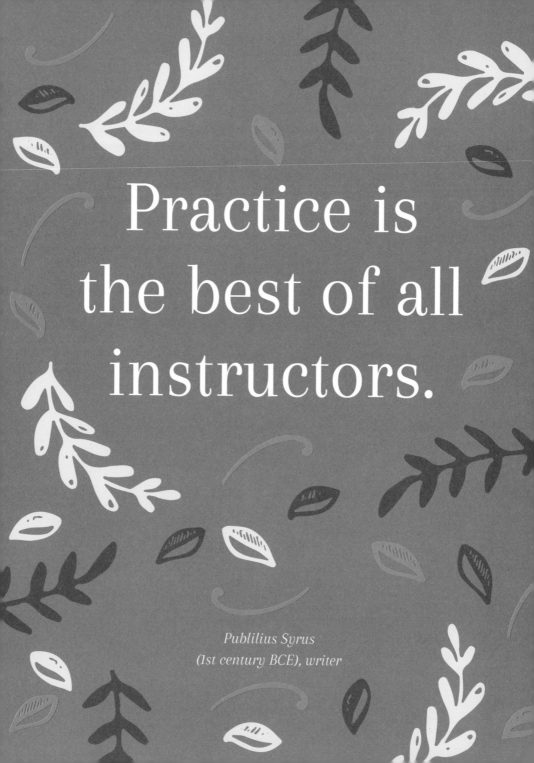

Practice is
the best of all
instructors.

*Publilius Syrus
(1st century BCE), writer*

Set a timer for five minutes. Sit quietly and take notice of these states:
physical, mental, and emotional. Afterward, write about it here.

Physical

_____

_____

_____

_____

_____

_____

_____

_____

Mental

_____

_____

_____

_____

_____

_____

_____

_____

Emotional

Pause and take a deep breath. There's no need to do anything in this moment—everything is OK just as it is.

Suggested Reading

There are so many wonderful books about acceptance, gratitude, and mindfulness. Here is a short list to get you started:

- *Radical Acceptance: Embracing Your Life with the Heart of a Buddha* by Tara Brach
- *When You're Falling, Dive: Acceptance, Freedom, and Possibility* by Cheri Huber
- *Get Out of Your Mind and Into Your Life: The New Acceptance and Commitment Therapy* by Steven C. Hayes and Spencer Smith
- *Stitches: A Handbook on Meaning, Hope, and Repair* by Anne Lamott
- *The Untethered Soul: The Journey Beyond Yourself* by Michael A. Singer

- *After the Ecstasy, the Laundry: How the Heart Grows Wise on the Spiritual Path* by Jack Kornfield
- *No Mud, No Lotus: The Art of Transforming Suffering* by Thich Nhat Hanh
- *When Things Fall Apart: Heart Advice for Difficult Times* by Pema Chödrön
- *Lovingkindness: The Revolutionary Art of Happiness* by Sharon Salzberg
- *The Gifts of Imperfection: Let Go of Who You Think You're Supposed to Be and Embrace Who You Are* by Brené Brown
- *Mindfulness in Plain English* by Bhante Gunaratana
- *Wherever You Go, There You Are: Mindfulness Meditation in Everyday Life* by Jon Kabat-Zin

About the Author

Before committing to the world of books, Anna Katz had a career in mental health and social services. As an editor and writer at Girl Friday Productions, she has worked with Nat Geo Kids, Deloitte, and Pokémon, among others. Her newest book, *Swimming Holes of Washington*, will be published by Mountaineers Books in 2018.

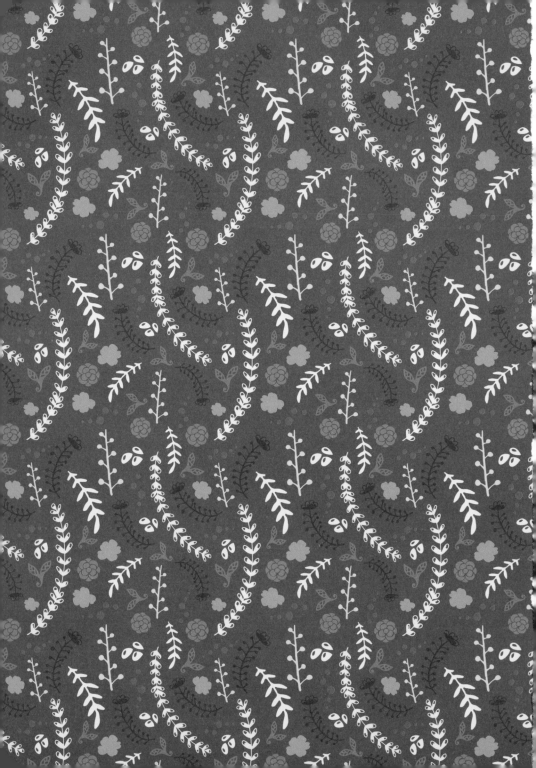